GENGHIS KHAN

demi

MARSHALL CAVENDISH CHILDREN

The story as contained within these pages is the author's interpretation of Genghis Khan's life based upon both historical resources and folklore.

Text and illustrations copyright © 1991 by Demi

First published in 1991 by Henry Holt and Company under the title *Chingis Khan*

Marshall Cavendish *Classics*

Marshall Cavendish is bringing classic titles from children's literature back into print for a new generation. We have selected titles that have withstood the test of time, and we welcome any suggestions for future titles in this program. To learn more, visit our Web site: www.marshallcavendish.us/kids.

Marshall Cavendish Corporation
99 White Plains Road
Tarrytown, NY 10591
www.marshallcavendish.us/kids

LIBRARY OF CONGRESS CATALOGING-IN-PUBLICATION DATA
Demi.
Genghis Khan / by Demi.
p. cm.
First ed. published in c1991 under title: Chingis Khan.
ISBN 978-0-7614-5547-9
1. Genghis Khan, 1162-1227—Juvenile literature. 2. Mongols—Kings and rulers—Biography—Juvenile literature. I. Demi. Genghis Khan. II. Title.
DS22.D46 2009
950'.21092—dc22
[B]
2008006001

Printed in China
First Marshall Cavendish Classics edition, 2009
1 3 5 6 4 2

BY THE BANKS OF THE ONON RIVER
in the year of the Snow Leopard, 1160,
a little boy was born. He would become
the greatest conqueror of all time.
His name was Temujin.

His father was called Yesugei and was the leader of the Yakka Mongols, which means Great Mongol Clan, one of the many clans in Mongolia.

Before he could walk, Temujin was strapped into a saddle and taught to ride on the vast Mongolian steppe.

When he was four, Temujin practiced archery with the other boys while riding at top speed. He could leap on his horse and maneuver in a flash, and at all times he was trained to watch the horizon for fast-striking raiders.

After archery practice, Temujin would play polo with his brothers and sisters—a game invented by the Mongols.

At five, Temujin herded vast numbers of Mongolian camels and goats and protected them from wolves. This taught him later in life how to maneuver and to protect large numbers of people.

The Mongolian camels were used for transportation and were known for their hardiness. They could sleep outdoors even in the coldest weather.

When Temujin was six, he was allowed to join the yearly hunt. The hunt was extremely dangerous. The Mongols formed a huge circle and drove the animals into the center where they were killed.

The most dangerous animals were the snow leopards, wolves, and the wild boars. The hunt made the boys skillful and fearless, and trained them to be wary as a wolf at all times. Later in life, Temujin used these skills to stalk and corner his enemies.

When Temujin was nine, his father Yesugei visited the Olkunut tribe to arrange Temujin's future marriage with a beautiful girl named Borte Ujin. On his return, Yesugei was poisoned by a jealous Tartar chief and died.

At nine, Temujin became
the head of the Yakka Mongols.
But most of the tribe deserted
him, feeling they could not be
protected by a mere child.

Temujin gathered those who remained into a small tribe and together they managed to subsist in one of the most desolate spots of Mongolia, living on roots, wild onions, and mice. No one thought Temujin's tribe would survive.

One day, Temujin caught his half brother Bekter stealing fish that was meant to feed the whole tribe. Because every bit of food counted, this act was a matter of life and death.

Temujin raised his bow and shot Bekter in the heart. Word of this deed spread to the outer steppes of Mongolia. It was said that Temujin was a stern and fierce leader.

One day, Temujin was chased by the Taichuit tribe. They were afraid of Temujin because he had "light in his eyes and fire on his face"—the face of a king! The Taichuits were afraid that he would lead the Yakka Mongols to power.

Temujin fled to the mountains where the forest was too thick for the Taichuits to follow. Temujin waited in the cold Khingan Mountains for many days.

On the ninth day, dizzy with cold and hunger, Temujin came out. He was immediately seized and bound in a yoke, or cangue. Temujin knew the following day he would be tortured to death.

While the Taichuits were feasting, Temujin used the only chance he had. He swung his cangue in a deadly arc that killed his guard and broke the cangue. Leaping onto a horse, he escaped into the night.

When the Taichuits discovered their prisoner was missing, the entire tribe charged after him and spotted his horse in the distance. Temujin jumped into the river and breathed through a straw reed, foiling his enemies once again.

As if by heaven sent, a Taichuit named Jelme appeared with a horse for Temujin and joined him in his escape. Jelme would become the first of Temujin's four great commanders.

Temujin led the way back to his little tribe, who had already heard of his daring escape. Stories of Temujin's bravery and fierce deeds spread among all the people. They said Temujin was steady, shrewd, and cautious in adversity. They said Temujin was brave and adventurous. They said he would become a mighty leader!

One day, two thieves drove off
eight of Temujin's nine horses.
This was a dangerous loss.
Temujin followed chase
on his last horse.

A herder named Borguchi showed Temujin the tracks of the thieves. Together they rode after them. Temujin shot the thieves, drove back the stolen horses, and many others as well.

Borguchi stayed by Temujin's side from that day on and would become the second of Temujin's four great commanders. Temujin was proving he could protect his small tribe. These acts of bravery and courage brought him still more followers.

One day during a snowstorm, a man named Subetei joined the tribe. He came in riding on a reindeer. Temujin, who could read people's faces and judge their characters, instantly knew this man was mighty indeed!

Subetei would become the third
of Temujin's four great commanders,
and the greatest of all his
Mongol warriors.

Temujin was seventeen when he married Borte Ujin of the Olkunut tribe. She wore a coat of white felt, white boots, gold coins in her hair, and a pine cone on top. And she carried a sheep, which was the symbol of plenty.

When the wedding chase started, Borte pretended to ride away and Temujin had to catch her and bring her back on his own horse. Children rode sheep, and everyone sang to celebrate this happy event.

That evening Temujin prayed to the Everlasting Blue Sky God, Bei Ulgan, for strength, wisdom, and power to protect all his people who lived in felt tents.

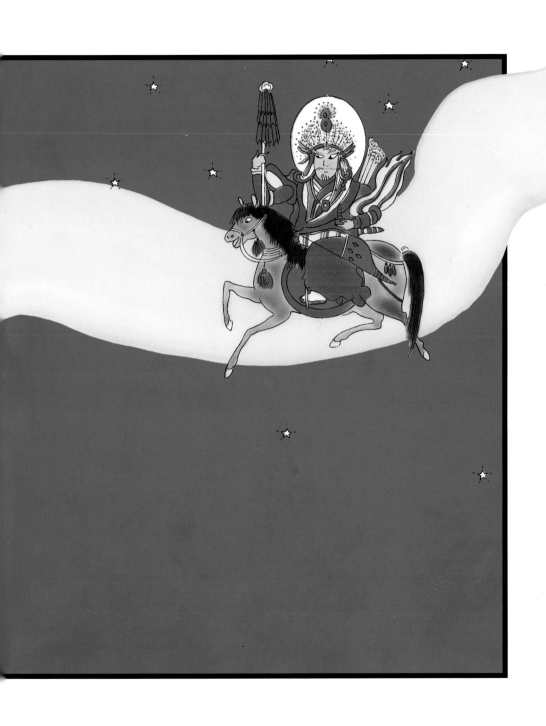

Bei Ulgan on his sky horse seemed to dance on the great northern lights as they lit up the vast Mongolian steppe. Temujin understood by this sign that he would unite the Mongols and conquer the world!

Soon hundreds of warriors from
far and wide joined Temujin's
tribe, bringing with them
their horses, wives, and children.

Everyone was talking about
Temujin's great courage, wisdom,
and ability to lead the people
who lived in felt tents.

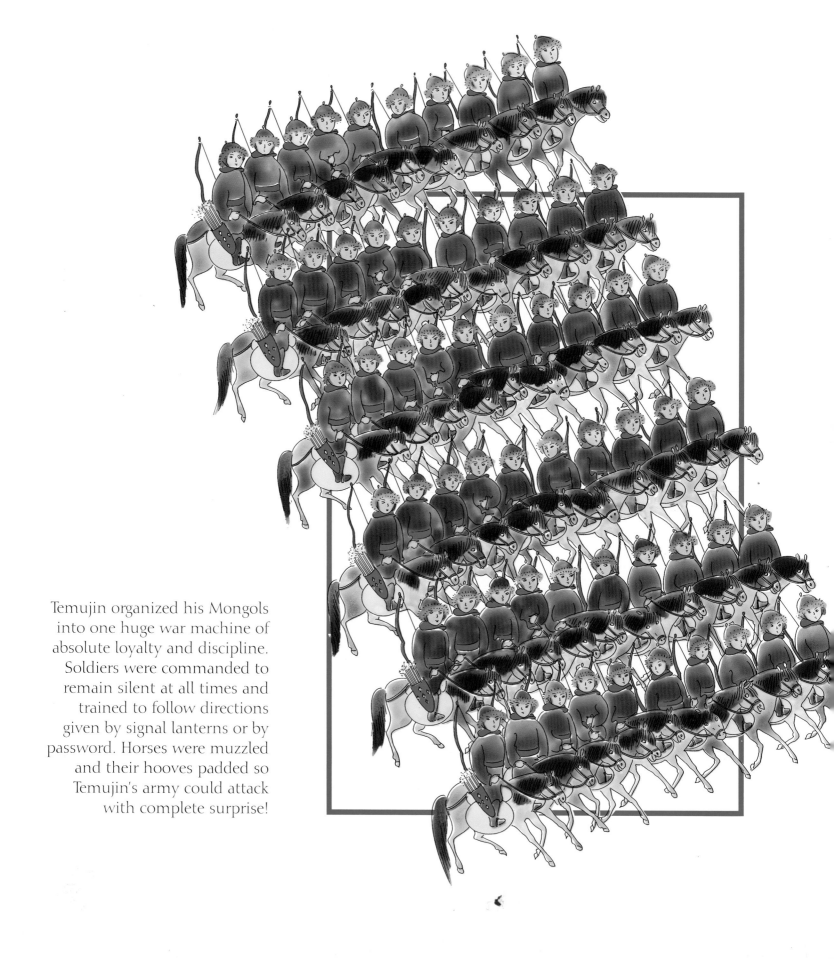

Temujin organized his Mongols into one huge war machine of absolute loyalty and discipline. Soldiers were commanded to remain silent at all times and trained to follow directions given by signal lanterns or by password. Horses were muzzled and their hooves padded so Temujin's army could attack with complete surprise!

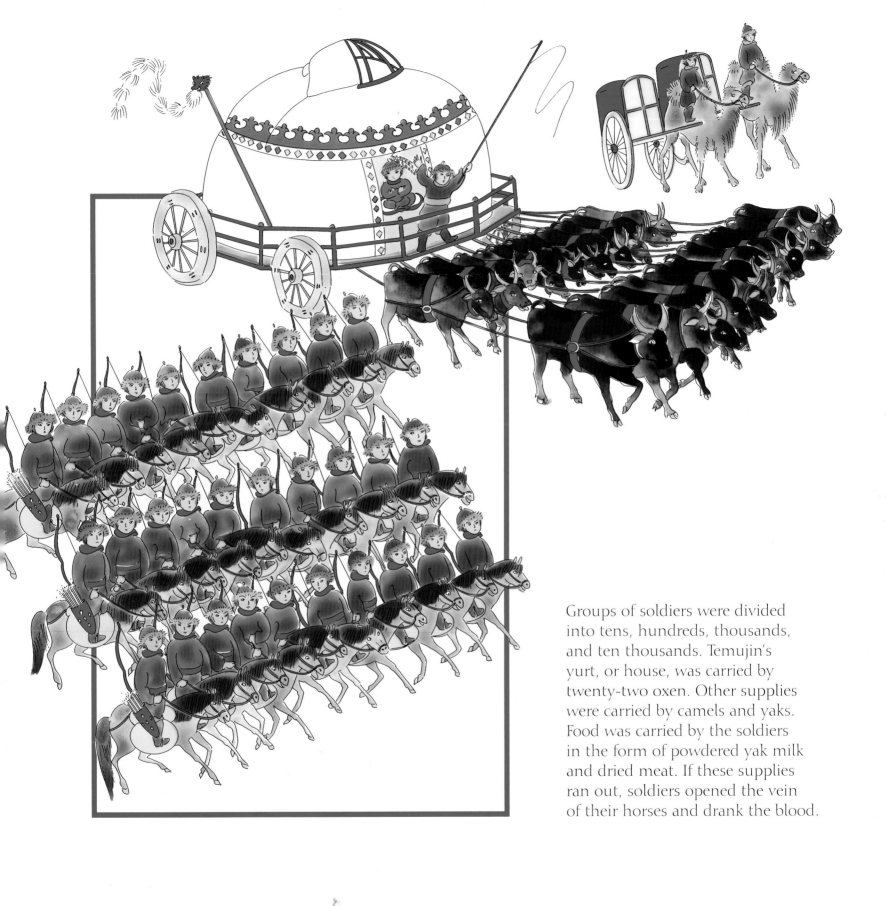

Groups of soldiers were divided into tens, hundreds, thousands, and ten thousands. Temujin's yurt, or house, was carried by twenty-two oxen. Other supplies were carried by camels and yaks. Food was carried by the soldiers in the form of powdered yak milk and dried meat. If these supplies ran out, soldiers opened the vein of their horses and drank the blood.

Temujin had united all the Mongolian tribes but one. The last and greatest was the Kerait. By ingenious warfare, Temujin forced their army to the top of a mountain. Anyone who tried to escape downhill was killed. During this battle, Temujin had noticed among the Keraits a most ferocious warrior who fought like a whirlwind. It seemed that he could shatter rocks and stop deep waters!

This warrior would die for his leader. And when he was captured, he expected death from Temujin. But Temujin admired loyalty above all. He pardoned the warrior and nicknamed him Chepe, which means *arrow*. This arrow—the fourth of Temujin's four great commanders—would gain him Persia, China, and Russia.

Jamunga, the leader of the fallen Keraits, had been a boyhood friend, so Temujin offered to spare his life. But both knew they were destined to be rivals and that there could be only one leader of all the Mongols.

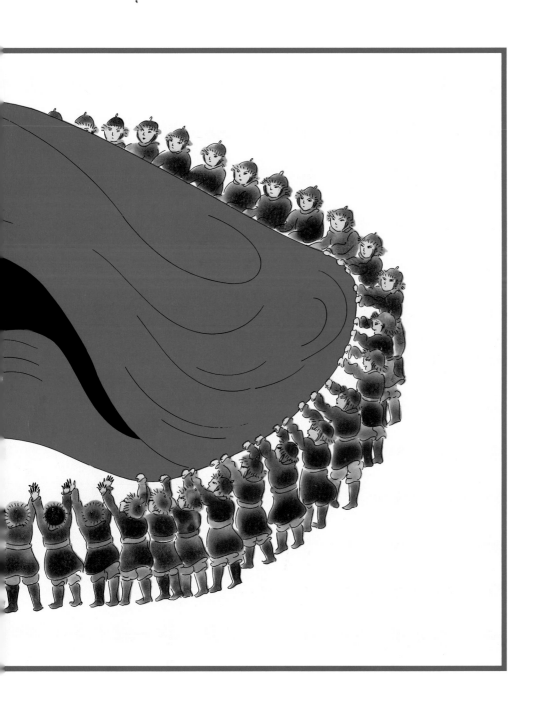

Jamunga therefore requested an honorable execution where no blood would be shed and his body would remain intact. Temujin granted this wish. Jamunga was beaten and suffocated between two blankets of felt. His spirit could then rise to the Everlasting Blue Sky and protect Temujin and all his people from above.

Temujin had defeated his last and greatest rival and unified the Mongols. In the year of the Snow Leopard, 1206, all the people who lived in felt tents assembled near the source of the Onon River. They raised the banner of nine white yak tails and proclaimed Temujin khan, or king. He was given the name Genghis which means *spirit of light*.

Genghis created a code of rules called the Yassa, based on customs of the steppe people. It demanded loyalty to one another, obedience, honesty, and discipline—and the merciless punishment of any wrongdoing. So well did the Yassa work that a cartload of gold and booty from military campaigns could be left unguarded, and no one would dare to touch it.

Now Genghis set out to conquer the world. First the Mongol army invaded Persia and captured every city that lay in its path. Balkh, Baghdad, Samarkand—all fell to Genghis!

He was so feared that the Persians said of him, "He is over eighteen feet tall, more powerful than three bulls, and one of his arrows can pierce twenty men!"

They said of his army, "They are leashed on an iron chain. Their skulls are of brass. Their teeth like chisels. Their hearts are of iron. Instead of whips they carry curved swords, drink dew, and ride with the wind!"

With each victory, Genghis gained knowledge of new methods of warfare. From the Persians he learned to use the "fire that flies."

After a victory Genghis would lecture his captives, telling them he was as powerful as fate. He paralyzed them with fear, saying, "I am an instrument of the wrath of Heaven!"

Genghis now wanted China and he attacked it from all sides, laid siege to cities, and tricked them into submission. The conquest of China was not easy, and it took him thirteen years to gain the title of Emperor of Heaven.

Genghis ordered Jelme, Borguchi, Subetei, and Chepe the Arrow to the West where they crushed everything in their path! Hungarian, Polish, and Russian cities were falling one after another to the invincible Mongols. Who knows how far they would have advanced?

Suddenly word came to them of the Great Khan's death in China, and the Mongols withdrew to rally round their dead khan. Genghis had died of a hunting wound inflicted by a wild boar.

When Genghis died in 1227 at the age of sixty-seven, it was at the height of his power, and he was the supreme master of the largest empire ever created in the lifetime of one man. He was buried near his birthplace, on a mountain that he loved. Once he had said, "It is so peaceful here that deer and birds come to rest—so will I."

When he was buried, the sky lit up with whirling lights that rose and fell and leapt like flames against the stars. The sky gods were dancing at the gate of the Heaven and as the spirit of Genghis entered, the earth trembled. Some fearful power had left the earth. Once again the earth trembled—then all was quiet. The mighty khan was gone.

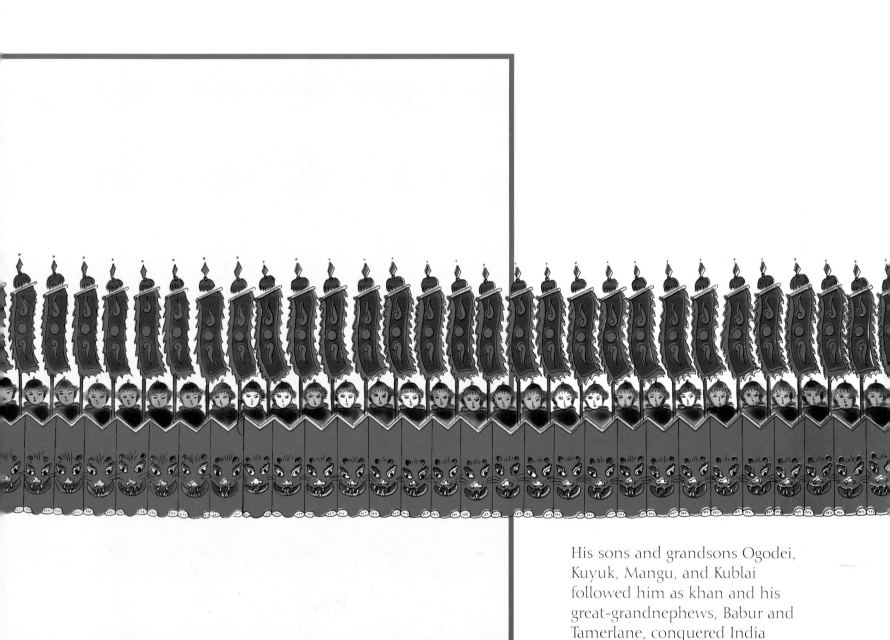

His sons and grandsons Ogodei,
Kuyuk, Mangu, and Kublai
followed him as khan and his
great-grandnephews, Babur and
Tamerlane, conquered India
and Asia in the tradition of
the mighty Genghis Khan.

Then the power of the Mongols
faded and vanished—
as a star at dawn,
as a flash of lightning
in a summer cloud,
as a phantom,
as a dream,
and as an illusion that is
mistaken for the real thing!